THE INFLUENCING POCKETBOOK

By Richard Storey

Drawings by Phil Hailstone

"Influence is the unseen lubricant in the engine of business; a management skill more vital than understanding finance and equally important for a business's balance sheet. Richard Storey is an expert in this field. His comprehensive coverage provides managers with the most complete quick reference guide available today."
Ed Lee, Training and Development Manager, BT Consulting & Systems Integration

"Provides extremely comprehensive guidance on a subject which many managers have difficulty with. It is well laid out so that it can be used as an introduction to influencing and for quick reference purposes prior to that difficult meeting."
Steve Ravenhill, Director of Human Resources, SunGard Availability Services (UK) Ltd

CONTENTS

PLANNING TO INFLUENCE

WHAT IS INFLUENCING?

Influencing is:

Getting your own way, especially unobtrusively.

Most managers do it, most of the time.

- You can influence others simply by being *you* (notice how easily children are influenced by the behaviour of those around them)
- You can influence covertly, behind the scenes
- You can use more open strategies and tactics

Great influencers manage to get other people to go along with their ideas while maintaining the relationship. If people feel manipulated, relationships will be damaged. It is important to understand the different strategies available to you and to plan your approach.

MASTERING THE ART

Increasingly, today's managers are measured by their ability to influence others at work. Being able to get people to do what you want has a direct effect on:

- The well-being of your staff
- The prosperity of your company
- And, ultimately, your own destiny

You are probably already successful at influencing others – some of the time.
How can you become consistently successful? If you can identify your strengths and weaknesses and make a few changes, nothing can hold you back.

What is the number one need for success in business today?

To persuade others of my value and the value of my ideas.

American Management Association
(from a survey of 2800 executives)

TYPICAL AREAS OF *OPEN* INFLUENCE

A lot of the time, especially in business, influencing is necessary and we accept it as part of human communication. It operates openly and usually follows a recognised process. Open influence can be seen in:

- Meetings
- Presentations
- Sales conversations
- Debates and discussions
- Change management
- Reports
- Proposals
- Negotiations
- Performance management
- Process management

TYPICAL AREAS OF *HIDDEN* INFLUENCE

Influence can also operate in a less open and direct manner. Your behaviour will be noticed by others, even though you are not necessarily trying to influence them. Your words will always be interpreted, however subtle or oblique. In short – whether we mean to influence or not – we are constantly beaming out influential messages to the world.

Hidden influence, which is often delicate, slow and on-going, works well in the following areas:

- Changing an image or behaviour
- Altering attitude
- Networking
- Communicating non-verbally
- Developing and maintaining rapport
- Nurturing relationships
- Counselling others
- Acting as a mentor
- Maintaining customer relations
- Using metaphor and analogy

WHAT MAKES AN EFFECTIVE INFLUENCER?

Winning influencers share attitudes and behaviours that ensure consistent success. Studies have shown that they:

I ndicate the benefits of their ideas

N eutralise resistance, preferably in advance

F ind alternative ways to influence others

L isten attentively to what others say

U ncover needs and wants

E mpathise continuously

N otice how others respond

C reate and maintain rapport throughout

E liminate weak statements from their language

R ehearse, rehearse, rehearse

PLANNING TO INFLUENCE

LIKELY OUTCOMES OF YOUR INFLUENCE

Most of the time, you will be seeking these outcomes:

- To maintain an existing positive relationship
- To gain commitment to your ideas
- To ensure your message is passed on to others

All influence gains some sort of reaction. On a scale of 1 to 5, these are the most likely responses you will receive.

1. Total commitment   *Terrific idea, wish I'd thought of it. When do we start?*
2. General agreement   *Not a bad idea. I've got one or two doubts.*
3. Compliance   *OK – you're the boss. I suppose we'd better start.*
4. Open disagreement   *This just won't work and here's why.*
5. Hidden sabotage   *(Thinks) You reckon it'll work; I'll prove you wrong.*

PLANNING TO INFLUENCE

KNOWING WHAT YOU WANT

Influencing is all about getting others to see things your way. Changing disagreement to agreement. But how do **they** see things? How far apart are your conflicting viewpoints – or is there some overlap?

Seeking areas of *mutual* agreement and amplifying these will automatically help you to minimise points of disagreement.

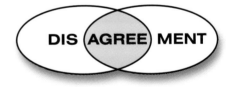

DIS AGREE MENT

By dovetailing your outcomes and recognising the needs of others, you immediately establish rapport. Rapport is the foundation of effective, long-lasting influence.

YOUR INFLUENCING OBJECTIVES

- Write down clearly and positively what you really want to achieve.

- Imagine what it will be like to achieve your outcome. What will it:
  - Look like?
  - Sound like?
  - Feel like?

- What is the context? Where, when, with whom?

- Is the outcome in your hands, or will you have to rely on others to make it happen?

- How might others be affected by your achievement? Are you happy with that?

9

5 EASY STEPS TO INFLUENCE

Here are the five main steps to effective influential communication. Make this pattern second nature, leaving you to concentrate on the detail.

1. Gain rapport
Be on their level; recognise their beliefs and values; match their behaviour patterns and blend your personality characteristics with theirs.

2. Ask questions
Elicit needs and different responses; probe to identify their motives, attitudes and feelings.

3. Listen actively
Demonstrate that you are listening; listen with all your senses; suspend judgement.

4. Stress pertinent benefits
Summarise how specific benefits of your proposal accurately reflect their needs.

5. Work towards a decision
Ask questions which will force a decision (or rejection); test interest through hypothetical questions; make positive statements which assume their acceptance.

5. Decision
4. Benefits
3. Listen
2. Questions
1. Rapport

BEHAVING AS IF YOU WILL SUCCEED

We are all influenced in some way by other people's behaviour. If they look and sound convincing, we are more likely to be influenced by them.

- Look the part; use positive body language to reinforce your messages
- Sound the part; underline your messages with the appropriate tone
- Avoid words that weaken the power of your messages
- Avoid unnecessary hesitation

Words that unintentionally weaken your message:

BELIEVE IN YOURSELF

Many people give up far too early. What if the great explorers, inventors, artists and politicians had thrown in the towel and gone home early? People who persevere recognise that early failure can provide helpful feedback.

- Experience + acceptance of failure = defeat and resignation
- Experience + review of feedback = learning, choice and growth

However, focusing too much effort on issues over which you have no influence or control can result in feelings of helplessness and powerlessness. The trick is to recognise that this is the case and back out gracefully.

PLANNING TO INFLUENCE

LUCK – OR GOOD PLANNING?

The golfer, Arnold Palmer,
was once told that he was really lucky.
'Yes,' he replied,
'and the more I practise,
the luckier I get.'

REHEARSE, REHEARSE, REHEARSE

The value of rehearsing complex influencing situations cannot be over emphasised.

1. Note your objectives
2. Find a suitable partner to role play with
3. Choose the actual location where you will be doing it for real
4. Brief your partner thoroughly
5. Practise one run through
6. Discuss the outcome and agree changes
7. Do a second run through
8. Discuss the outcome
9. Repeat as often as needed
10. Go in to the actual scenario with great confidence!

INFLUENCING STYLES

INFLUENCING STYLES

THE FLEXIBLE MANAGER

The way in which you behave as a manager and the approach you take will have a marked effect on your ultimate success or failure.

Having a range of approaches and styles of behaviour gives you more flexibility.

It increases your options - and your chance of success.

Keep on doing what you always do
and you'll always get what you always got.

NATURAL STYLES

Most managers have a natural style of influence which they prefer to use whenever possible. More flexible managers also keep in reserve a fall back style, used when the preferred style doesn't achieve the desired results.

However, there are at least eight identifiable styles of influence - not including aggression, manipulation or force!

Because you are influencing a wide range of people, proficiency in a wider range of styles will ensure more success. Step outside the comfort zone of your natural style and enjoy greater success by practising new ways of influencing.

Beware: think carefully which influencing style has the greatest chance of succeeding. Varying your styles too much may give you a reputation for being unpredictable.

THE AUTOCRATIC, PUSH APPROACH

You tell 'em, they agree.

Use the push style when:

- You are looking for a quick response
- You seek only short-term commitment
- You are happy to check up and follow through

This approach works best when supported by
power, authority, age, knowledge or wisdom.
Resistance or objections are minimised.
You tell others what you want them to do.

Health Warning: Autocracy can
be a high-risk strategy. It may
result in a feeling of 'You won, I lost'.
They'll get you next time.

INFLUENCING STYLES

THE COLLABORATIVE, PULL APPROACH

You include others in the decision-making process.

Use the pull style when:

- You want to maintain long-term influence with others
- You seek a high level of commitment
- You have no time to enforce the outcome

This approach works successfully without you having any power or authority.

Health Warning: Democracy takes time and can result in watered down solutions. Remain consistently collaborative. Don't give up too early. Avoid imposing too many parameters or conditions – these will create frustration in others.

19

THE LOGICAL APPROACH

You use clear, logical, unassailable arguments, supported by proof.

Use logic when:

- The other person demands evidence and lots of detail
- You are prepared to do your homework
- You are prepared to wait for a reaction

This approach works best when the other person is a logical, linear thinker. Avoid exaggeration and unnecessary emotion. Offer instead facts and figures.

Health Warning: You may find this style long-winded and frustrating. You may even be forced to put it in writing. Allow time to prepare your argument, time to explain it, time to wait for a reaction.

THE EMOTIONAL APPROACH

You use your natural charm, charisma or enthusiasm.

Use emotion when:

- You want others to feel part of an exciting project
- You want to fire up someone's motivation
- You are truly enthusiastic about an idea

This approach works well when your influence becomes a genuine extension of your own feelings and beliefs. Appealing to the long-term effects of your ideas, you will reinforce their continuing value.

Health Warning: Emotional appeal carries risks. It can leave a nasty taste in the mouth. Painful memories linger longer.

THE ASSERTIVE APPROACH

You ask directly, clearly and confidently for what you want, or don't want.

Be assertive when:

- You want to influence autocratic people, bullies, stick-in-the-muds
- You want to influence behaviours
- You need to act and initiate, rather than react

Assertiveness can have a lasting effect, especially on those who least expect it from you.
Any resistance is met by your persistence.

 Health Warning: None. Assertive influence carries little or no risk.

THE PASSIVE APPROACH

You win the day by being submissive,
by not overtly influencing.

Remain passive when:

- You want to influence others through
  personal demonstration

- You want to avoid unhelpful confrontation

- You have tried all the other approaches

As you quietly demonstrate desired behaviours, others
can see for themselves the value in following your
lead. Many potential confrontations with power or
authority demand submissive influence,
which can pay positive dividends.

 Health Warning: Your submissiveness may leave
you with feelings of low self-esteem. Can you live with this?

THE SALES APPROACH

You use good, old-fashioned salesmanship.

Use salesmanship when:

- You know that the other person expects to be sold to
- You need to show the benefits your suggestion will produce
- You enjoy selling your ideas

Draw out their point of view; understand their needs; demonstrate that you empathise; minimise resistance by showing how their ideas dovetail with your own; show how they will benefit.

 Health Warning: Logical or submissive people often hate an overt sales approach and may work hard to wreck your plans.

THE BARGAINING APPROACH

You trade concessions in order to reach a mutually acceptable conclusion.

Bargain or negotiate when:

- You are both equally keen to go ahead with the idea
- You are happy and able to offer a few concessions
- You want to reach a *win-win* conclusion

Don't just share the cake – make it a bigger one. Your success as a fair negotiator will help cement the relationship.

✚ Health Warning: Aim too low and you'll end up even lower. Over collaborate and you may regret giving too much away. Always *trade* concessions.

THE POWER OF POSITIVE BEHAVIOUR (1)

Who has been a big influence in your life? A parent, relative, employer, friend or neighbour? Chances are that they often did nothing specific to influence you – they just behaved in ways that you took note of and decided to copy.

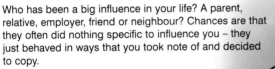

The behaviour of others can be influenced greatly when they observe the ways in which you:

- Deal with aggression
- Handle awkward customers
- Control group behaviour
- Field tricky questions
- Overcome resistance
- Live by your values and beliefs
- Walk the talk

INFLUENCING STYLES

THE POWER OF POSITIVE BEHAVIOUR (2)

Behaviours that help the influencing process:

- Continuous maintenance of rapport
- Maintaining good eye contact
- Congruent body language which supports your messages
- Appropriate voice tone which underpins what you say
- Sensory acuity – noticing how others react to you and your messages
- Flexibility – being prepared to change your approach, where necessary
- Awareness and acceptance of the needs of others
- Lack of words that weaken your messages

MODELLING BEHAVIOUR

OK, suppose you don't have sufficient flexibility of style. With practice, it's easy to observe, analyse and reproduce the effective behaviours of other people. If you've ever studied any skill under a master, you will already have done this.

Suppose you know a person who uses an influencing style in a particularly elegant or effective manner. You have identified this as something you would like to improve for yourself. By closely observing what works for that person and noticing the effect it has on others, you can begin to experiment by adopting these behaviours and strategies, and making them work for you, too. Behaviour is only behaviour – it can usually be replicated.

WHAT'S IN IT FOR ME?

WHAT MAKES PEOPLE SAY *YES*?

When we agree to an idea or proposal, it's because there's something in it for us.
It's hard to influence people who can't see what's in it for them. Sounds one-sided, but it
is true. Call it self-interest, greed, selfishness or whatever. It is only human nature to ask,
'What am I getting from this?'.

People will say *yes* to your ideas if they meet their needs or match their view of life in the
following areas:

- Principles and values
- Beliefs and opinions
- Needs and wants

WHAT'S IN IT FOR ME?

GIVE PEOPLE WHAT THEY WANT & NEED

I love strawberries.
But whenever I go fishing
I bait my hook with worms.
This is because fish like
worms – not strawberries.

Dale Carnegie

PRINCIPLES & VALUES

People agree to ideas and suggestions that match their needs or views of life. Underpinning all our lives are certain principles and values that we hold to be true. These become guidelines for how we conduct our lives. They influence and mould our behaviour. They can differ greatly from person to person and successful influencers always take principles and values into account.

But how?
- Notice what principles and values drive other people
- Ask questions and invite comment and reaction
- Check with those who know them well

Some examples of principles:
'Integrity and fairness are an integral part of business dealings.'
'I think that older people deserve courtesy and consideration.'
'Moral behaviour is part of the fabric of daily life.'
It would be unproductive to spend time attempting to dislodge these deep-seated principles. Instead, harness them to add leverage to your suggestions.

BELIEFS & OPINIONS

Beliefs and opinions can be transient or short-term. Remember when you used to believe in Father Christmas, the Tooth Fairy, giants and witches? Proof can easily dislodge a belief. So, too, can time.

An early step on the road to influencing others may include having to change lingering beliefs or convictions before you can proceed further.

'I think that SpeedClean washing machines break down more often than the Tumbleboy range.'

'I think that all politicians are corrupt.'

'I never make decisions on the 13th.'

Each of these beliefs can be dealt with by using a SuperQuestion (see page 43) or providing proof or data.

WHAT'S IN IT FOR ME?

NEEDS & NECESSITIES

These are fundamental requirements – they have to be met if you are to influence others.

Typical needs include: reliability, security, achieving a deadline, meeting a budget, keeping up to date.

'Because of increasing competition, it is essential that we maintain an image and at the same time keep up to date.'

'My team members are under great pressure, so it is important to maintain their morale.'

'The system must not only be reliable but secure, as well.'

Having uncovered needs, you may have to mould or reshape your ideas to dovetail with the requirements of others.

Often, people have a hierarchy of needs, so it may be important to discover and use this: 'Which is most important to you – reliability or security?'.

WANTS & WISHES

Wants and wishes are not essentials,
just a wish list: 'Wouldn't it be lovely …
if only'. But their fulfilment can be the cherry
on your influencing trifle, placed on top with
a flourish, after the other person has agreed
to your proposal.

WHAT'S IN IT FOR ME?

DEPENDS WHAT'S ON OFFER

Question: *How will your suggestions benefit the other person?*

The person or people you are influencing will interpret the benefits of your suggestions in different ways. Some will be interested in the features – the fine details, the nitty gritty of your ideas. Others will say 'How will I benefit?'. Others will seek out the advantages of your proposals – how the benefits are different.

People don't buy a new detergent because of the manufacturer. They buy it because it promises a benefit.

David Ogilvy, advertising legend

FEATURES, BENEFITS & ADVANTAGES

Features
These are built-in aspects of your idea or suggestion – timing, costs, resources and so on. They will remain locked up in your idea whether the other person agrees or not.

Benefits
These are far more important than the features of your proposal. They translate boring old features into exciting statements which show clearly how others will gain.

'This new hardware is made in Sweden (feature) which means that we will save time and money on spare parts (benefit).'

Advantages
These are comparative benefits – more money, greater savings, faster turn-round.

WHAT'S IN IT FOR ME?

THE BENEFIT BALANCE SHEET

Most people do not agree whole-heartedly to an idea. There is usually something that niggles, however well you've addressed their concerns.

In the end, when we finally say *yes* to a proposal, it is because the benefits outweigh any disadvantages.

As you plan and prepare your influencing case, list all the benefits and advantages of your suggestion. Use them to tip the balance in favour of *yes*.

COMMUNICATING
YOUR MESSAGE

GAINING ENTRY

Where do you start? What do you say first? How do you gain attention?
Just like a game of chess, the first moves are often vital to the outcome of the match.
Think carefully about the impact of your opening gambit.

Often, you will need to build the case for your idea gradually, particularly if the other person is initially resistant. The model below will help you to remember the stages in opening a discussion and building need.

O utcome questions – often assumptive but designed to reveal a desired outcome for the other person: 'How would you like to see this improved?'.

P roblem questions – designed to elicit the problems connected with the outcome: 'What would it cost to improve it?'.

E xploration questions – designed to show the implication of the problems: 'Is it lack of resources which prevents you from making changes?'.

N eed questions - designed to bring them to the conclusion that they have a need for your proposal: 'So, if we can find other ways of saving money, it would fund the project and we could go ahead. Do you agree?'.

COMMUNICATING YOUR MESSAGE

THE OPENING GAMBIT

Much influence can be lost or dissipated in the first few sentences. With careful thought (and, if necessary, rehearsal) you can set the climate, elicit responses and identify a need within your opening gambit.

Imagine that a colleague has recently been making errors and you want to examine systems and procedures that may have contributed to the mistakes. You expect some resistance as the systems were designed by the same colleague. An opening gambit may go something like this:

'Sam, I know you and your team are under a lot of pressure at present and I have an idea which could help relieve some of it for you. Interested? Good. Your system has worked well in the past but recent changes have affected the way it operates. I expect you have noticed some errors in the sales returns for last quarter? Right. Well, I think we can kill two birds with one stone – adjust the system and remove the errors ...'

POWER WORDS

Some words and phrases are more potent or compelling than others. The way you shape your message can affect the response you get.

Here are some powerful winning words – pepper your conversation with them (or use them in writing) and notice their effect on others:

Security	New	Enjoy
Safety	Best	Save
Guaranteed	Evidence	Convenient
Reliable	Research	Easy
Tested	Logical	Trouble free
Proven	Fun	Inexpensive
Unique	Tried	Free

INTRODUCING SUPERQUESTIONS

To take someone where you want them to go, you have to know where they are at the moment. To influence their ideas, you have to know what those ideas are.

Language is a powerful filter on our experiences. It channels our thoughts and preserves mindsets. Most commonly, our choice of words can create:

- Lazy language; we assume that others know what we mean when we use a noun or a verb, or make comparisons

- Limiting language; seemingly insurmountable barriers can be raised with words such as *can't, should not, must not, never, always*

Successful influencers use *SuperQuestions* to exploit the strengths and minimise the weaknesses of language. *SuperQuestions* unravel the meaning of another person's map and help reconnect the words they use with their experience. They have maximum leverage by using language to clarify language.

DEALING WITH LAZY LANGUAGE

Deletions are examples of language where parts of the meaning have been omitted, accidentally or for a purpose.

- Nouns that mean nothing to you
- Imprecise verbs
- Verbs that have been turned into vague nouns
- Unspecified comparisons

SuperQuestions quickly and easily enable the speaker to reconnect their words to omitted or unspecified meaning.

SUPERQUESTIONS THAT CLARIFY

These *SuperQuestions* challenge a deletion by uncovering the detail behind a statement and reconnecting the speaker with the reality of their experience. You can review, focus and expand an individual's thinking by gathering more detailed, or specific, information.

'I am never allowed to make *decisions*.'
SuperQuestion: 'What *kind* of decisions are you not allowed to make?'

'I hate *contracts*.'
SuperQuestion: 'Which *contracts* exactly?'

'She needs to *improve* her influencing skills.'
SuperQuestion: 'In what way does she need to *improve?*'

'My boss *annoyed* me.'
SuperQuestion: 'How exactly did your boss *annoy* you?'

'All I want is a little *recognition*.'
SuperQuestion: 'How *precisely* would you like to be recognised?'

'System *security* is all important.'
SuperQuestion: 'In what ways do you want to *secure* the system?'

'My presentation was *really bad*.'
SuperQuestion: 'Compared with what?'

'She's the *best* person for the job.'
SuperQuestion: '*Better* than whom, specifically?'

DEALING WITH LIMITING LANGUAGE

Apparent rules, limitations and generalisations can be misleading and often seem to prevent or block possibilities.

- *We must not … we should …*
- *I can't …*
- *I always … we never …*
- *That's not possible …*
- *I just don't know the reason why …*

46

SUPERQUESTIONS THAT CHALLENGE LIMITATIONS

These *SuperQuestions* challenge limitations (often self-imposed or imaginary). They also allow the other person to discover and explore alternative ways forward.

'We *mustn't* do it that way.'
SuperQuestion: 'What would happen if we did?'

'You *should* keep a copy.'
SuperQuestion: 'What would happen if we didn't?'

'I *can't* do that right now.'
SuperQuestion: 'I can understand your difficulty but what exactly is preventing you from doing it?'

'We *never* promote people in their first year.'
SuperQuestion: 'Has there ever been an occasion when you did promote someone?'

'That's just *not possible*. More than my job's worth …etc, etc.'
SuperQuestion: 'What would have to happen to make it possible?'

'I *don't know* the reason.'
SuperQuestion: 'If you did know the reason, take a guess at what it could be.'

'I *always* use the XYZ Company.'
SuperQuestion: 'Has there ever been a time when you didn't?'

COMMUNICATING YOUR MESSAGE

WHEN TO USE SUPERQUESTIONS

SuperQuestions are powerful. Like any power tool, they can be hurtful and dangerous to use.

Think carefully before you use a *SuperQuestion*. Ask yourself these questions:

- Will a *SuperQuestion* really help clarify the meaning?
- Can I still maintain rapport while using a *SuperQuestion*?
- Am I over-using *SuperQuestions*?

SOFTENING YOUR SUPERQUESTIONS

SuperQuestions have been likened to a scalpel that cuts cleanly and quickly through linguistic fluff. You are asking people to see things from a new or different perspective – a process which, for some, can be difficult, painful or annoying.

Phrases that preface and soften the immediate effect of a *SuperQuestion* include:

- *I can see your point of view and …*
- *Hmm … I think I know what you mean …*
- *Yes, I've often thought that and …*

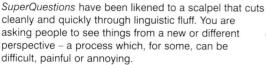

COMMUNICATING YOUR MESSAGE

NOW JUST LISTEN TO ME

Effective and flexible influencers are also good listeners.

Listening with care is a rare skill. Many people use up valuable listening time by:

- Trying to re-enter the conversation
- Thinking out the next response or argument
- Mentally disagreeing with the speaker
- Making evaluations and judgements
- Allowing their minds to wander
- Looking away from the speaker
- Allowing noise or other
  conversation to distract

Listening is the highest form of courtesy.

Tom Peters

WHOLE BODY LISTENING

Whole body listening is listening with total
rapport and empathy. It is giving the whole of
your attention to the speaker. It is having the
ability to focus your attention externally and not
thinking your own thoughts.

- Listen with your ears
- Listen with your eyes
- Listen with your heart

COMMUNICATING YOUR MESSAGE

LISTEN WITH YOUR EARS

Listening to the words and how they come across will enable you to step into another person's world.

- How does the other person articulate what he or she says?

- How does the speaker describe his or her reality?

- What is the person's belief system?

- What tone of voice does the speaker use?

- Is the tone congruent with the message conveyed by the words?

- Is the person speaking quietly or loudly, fast or slow?

LISTENING WITH YOUR EYES

Eye contact is a vital ingredient of listening. But just focusing your eyes on the speaker does not mean that you are listening.

Notice the speaker's face, eyes, mouth, body posture.

Look out for subtle changes in:

- Skin colour
- Muscle tension and relaxation
- The rate of breathing
- Posture and gesture

All of this can endorse what is said (or spell out a different message) and let you know what effect your influence is having.

COMMUNICATING YOUR MESSAGE

LISTENING WITH YOUR HEART

As you hear the words spoken by the other person, begin to notice ways in which you can empathise with what is being said and how it is expressed. You can gain valuable insights into what is being thought and felt.

To influence with empathy, you will need to know where the other person is coming from. Then, lead them gently towards where you would like them to be.

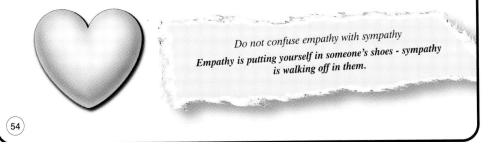

Do not confuse empathy with sympathy
Empathy is putting yourself in someone's shoes - sympathy is walking off in them.

COMMUNICATING YOUR MESSAGE

NOISES OFF

When someone is speaking to you face to face, begin to notice how much of the time is spent looking away from you. The speaker is recalling an event in his or her mind's eye, searching for the right words, or reliving an emotion.

As speakers can spend as much as 80 – 90% of the time looking away, use these moments to enhance your listening. When we listen on the telephone we don't remain silent. To avoid speakers thinking they have been disconnected, we beef up our listening by making sounds to show that we are hanging on to their every word.

These sounds are called *noises off*. And they can be used just as effectively in a face to face chat.

COMMUNICATING YOUR MESSAGE

NOISES OFF

On the telephone you demonstrate that you are listening by making noises:

- Uh, huh, mmm
- Really?
- Oh
- Phew!
- Wow
- Laughter
- Whistle
- Intake of breath

In face to face conversations these sounds also provide a valuable clue to speakers that you are listening while they look away from you. They add a further dimension to the underrated art of listening.

INFLUENCING THROUGH RAPPORT

INFLUENCING THROUGH RAPPORT

WHAT EXACTLY IS RAPPORT?

Rapport is the most important process in influencing others. It is vital if you want to maintain the relationship. Without it, you are unlikely to achieve willing agreement to what you want. People who have excellent rapport with others create harmonious relationships based on trust and understanding of mutual needs.

Rapport is the cornerstone of all mutually effective relationships. It needs constant vigilance and nurturing to keep it alive and effective.

Until you let me be an 'I' the way you are,
you can never come inside my silence and know me.

From the film *Children of a Lesser God*

58

INFLUENCING THROUGH RAPPORT

WHY IS IT SO IMPORTANT?

Rapport is similar to money – when you are short of it, it increases in importance.
Without rapport you will reduce your chances of getting:

- Unconditional agreement to your ideas and suggestions
- Full commitment from others
- Business, promotion, friends

The way in which you interact with others has a major bearing on your success
as an influencer.

Being in rapport means that you are in agreement with others both verbally
and non-verbally.

INFLUENCING THROUGH RAPPORT

TEN GOOD REASONS TO BUILD RAPPORT

1. To really win friends and influence people
2. To connect rapidly with a wide range of people
3. To communicate magically
4. To build solid, lasting relationships
5. To create incredible results
6. To help others improve performance and increase success
7. To handle conflict
8. To get promotion
9. To talk your way in to things
10. To talk your way out of things

A RECIPE FOR SUCCESSFUL INFLUENCING

Ingredients:

Trust
Openness
Comfort
Acceptance
Empathy
Flexibility
Something in common
Shared understanding

Method:

Mix together as required. Notice changes and be prepared to maintain a flexible approach throughout. Keep communication flowing on all levels.

SELF-DISCLOSURE

Telling others how you feel and what you think and believe, as well as telling them about your background, is a kind of currency. Give out information and usually you will receive a lot back in return.

People swarm, flock and group together by type, background, interests, beliefs, gender, work and so on. And one of the most efficient ways to get close to one another is through self-disclosure.

As we begin to experience a powerful common bond, so too does rapport begin. Mutual interests, ideas, values and beliefs are the warp and weft of social interaction.

Most people like people who are like themselves.

BIOGRAPHIC MATCHING

It is rare for two human beings to be together very long before seeking to discover similarities about themselves. This biographic matching can be social or economic, achieved through outlook, education or background – common experiences of the world.

When you match, you reduce resistance by playing down differences while building on similarities.

INFLUENCING THROUGH RAPPORT

PACING

Once you are matching one another, you can continue to maintain the rhythm you have created by agreeing with one another, seeing things from the same point of view. Pacing is a conscious continuation of matching.

When talking, you can pace:

- Words that are used
- Tone of voice
- Rate of speech
- Language patterns
- Volume
- Body language used

Warning: Don't overdo it – you may be accused of mimicry. Be elegant – your skills should remain unnoticed.

INFLUENCING THROUGH RAPPORT

LEADING

One of the goals of matching and pacing others is to be able effortlessly to lead them in another direction. Once you are deeply in sync. with the other person, a change of pace from you will usually result in a similar change in others.

Matching and pacing help you share someone else's experience and you will begin to know intuitively when it is appropriate to make suggestions, to influence, to lead.

It is much easier, and much more effective, to move from agreement to agreement than from disagreement to agreement

Jerry Richardson

65

INFLUENCING THROUGH RAPPORT

MISMATCHING

You can also influence behaviour in others by *mismatching*. It is useful to mismatch when:

- You want a meeting to come to an end – clear up papers, put a pen away
- You want to conclude a telephone conversation – minimise responses and noises off
- You need time to think before acting – use the bathroom, make a telephone call, add up figures on your calculator
- What you are doing isn't working – go for a walk, listen to some music, make a phone call
- Matching is affecting your mood negatively – break off the conversation, change the subject

NETWORKING

Have you noticed how some people seem to be universally liked, trusted and respected? Chances are that they're also good at networking – developing a wide network of friends, colleagues, allies and useful contacts.

Networking offers you a structured way of making certain that your ideas are effectively exchanged with others.

> *Two thirds of all European business deals worth more than £6.5 million are agreed over a game of golf.*

Kapital, a German economics journal

INFLUENCING THROUGH RAPPORT

NETWORKING IN ACTION

How can you get to know your team, other managers and clients better? Are there management associations you could join, luncheon clubs, your local Chamber of Commerce?

Organise team events outside working hours. Be seen at functions, offer to assist whenever you can.

Make yourself known – don't stand on the edge looking in. Be part of the action.

INFLUENCING DIFFERENT PERSONALITIES

FLEXIBLE BEHAVIOUR

We do not all have the same personality. Sometimes we get on instantly with other people, occasionally there's a clash. Changing your behaviour to suit different people is perfectly normal. It doesn't change you as an individual, nor is it manipulative.

What you are sounds so loudly in my ears that I cannot hear what you say.

Ralph Waldo Emerson

THE FOUR TYPES

The model here shows four different personality 'types'.

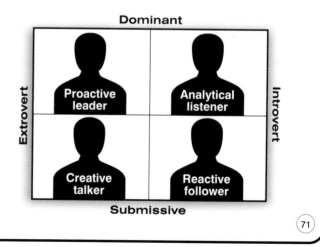

IDENTIFYING THE PROACTIVE LEADER

Positive characteristics:

- Planner
- Goal setter
- Disciplined
- Organised
- Open to new ideas
- Enjoys using power
- Appears confident and authoritative
- Task oriented
- Makes fast decisions
- Can be kind and helpful

INFLUENCING DIFFERENT PERSONALITIES

IDENTIFYING THE PROACTIVE LEADER

Negative points:

- Insensitive
- Easily bored
- Aggressive
- Overbearing
- Impatient
- Blunt
- Ruthless
- A poor delegator
- Conscious of status
- Materialistic

(73)

INFLUENCING THE PROACTIVE LEADER

Present your ideas in ways that boost the person's prestige. Genuine praise can work wonders. Use power words such as: best, biggest, unique, powerful, fast, money, first. Go for a decision, quickly and often.

THE ANALYTICAL LISTENER

Positive characteristics:

- Thorough
- Calm
- Good listener
- Rational
- Logical
- Loves statistics of all types
- Formal and disciplined
- Thoughtful
- Subtle
- Deliberate

THE ANALYTICAL LISTENER

Negative characteristics:

- Makes slow decisions
- Procrastinates
- Closed to new ideas
- Hates overt persuasion
- Searches for inaccuracies
- Slow to trust
- Distant and unemotional
- Bureaucratic
- Demands evidence
- Requires guarantees

INFLUENCING DIFFERENT PERSONALITIES

INFLUENCING THE ANALYTICAL LISTENER

Like the proactive leader, this person is strongly independent. Don't rush things – plan to give the person plenty of breathing space and thinking time. If your suggestions stack up, the person will come round to your way of thinking. Putting everything in writing (along with lots of juicy statistics) can be a good idea. Above all, don't even think about conning this type of person – it will be spotted instantly.

Power words that work well include: proof, evidence, facts and figures, research, logic, tried and tested, safe, reason.

THE REACTIVE FOLLOWER

Positive characteristics:

- Good listener
- Dependable
- Friendly
- Loyal
- Passive
- Gentle
- Thoughtful
- People oriented
- Quiet
- Easily influenced!

THE REACTIVE FOLLOWER

Negative characteristics:

- Cautious
- Submissive
- Slow to trust
- Requires proof
- Relies on outside approval
- Hates pressure
- Dislikes change

INFLUENCING THE REACTIVE FOLLOWER

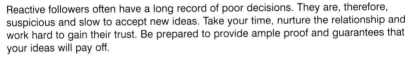

Reactive followers often have a long record of poor decisions. They are, therefore, suspicious and slow to accept new ideas. Take your time, nurture the relationship and work hard to gain their trust. Be prepared to provide ample proof and guarantees that your ideas will pay off.

Power words that work well include: security, safety, guaranteed, reliable, popular, tried and tested, fail-safe, proven.

THE CREATIVE TALKER

Positive characteristics:

- Responsive
- Talkative
- Very sociable
- Friendly
- Good listener
- Impulsive
- Creative
- Relishes new ideas
- Enthusiastic
- Makes rapid decisions

THE CREATIVE TALKER

Negative characteristics:

- Undisciplined
- Poor timekeeper
- Disorganised
- Lazy
- Impulsive
- Gullible and easily led
- Impatient
- Emotional
- Nostalgic
- Over generalises

INFLUENCING THE CREATIVE TALKER

These people like to be liked and appreciated. They need people around them and are anxious to develop and maintain relationships. Be prepared to steer and control the conversation.

Power words that work well include: fun, appreciate, enjoy, convenient, trouble-free, inexpensive.

NOTES

HANDLING RESISTANCE

HANDLING RESISTANCE

WHY DO PEOPLE RESIST & OBJECT?

To handle resistance to your ideas and influence, you will first need to pinpoint exactly why there is an objection. Typically, people object or resist because they:

- Don't fully understand your proposal
- Misunderstand it
- Don't feel a need to go ahead
- Don't recognise the benefits and advantages
- Don't believe your claims
- Are happy to remain as they are
- Genuinely need time to think things through
- Don't trust you
- Display general inertia

WHAT TYPE OF RESISTANCE?

Objections and resistance usually come in three identifiable forms:

A condition is a genuine, non-negotiable reason why someone can't go ahead or agree to your proposal (eg: company policy, legal reasons, a contractual obligation).

An excuse or a put-off is usually made because people are not convinced of the benefits of your ideas. Excuses cannot be answered – conviction is the only solution.

A real objection can include lack of money or resources, time constraints, happiness with the status quo.

Give us the serenity to accept what cannot be changed, the courage to change what should be changed - and the wisdom to distinguish the one from the other.

Rhienhold Niebuhr

HANDLING RESISTANCE

STRATEGIES & TACTICS

Resistance can be very frustrating. You are anxious to get on with things and it is hard to see why others are stonewalling. This is the moment to back off and take stock.

1. Listen carefully to what they are saying to you.
2. Watch their body language – does it contain any hidden messages?
3. Step into their shoes; try to see things from their point of view.
4. Consider what would have to happen for *you* to be convinced?
5. Plan your responses carefully.
6. Take time to construct carefully thought through responses.
7. Check that you have provided acceptable responses to doubts and fears.
8. Seek areas of agreement and stress them; minimise areas of disagreement.

CATEGORIES OF RESISTANCE

It is not enough to know whether people are for or against you and your ideas and proposals. The people you want to influence can be divided into ten categories.

Those who:
1. Covertly disagree
2. Openly disagree
3. Comply - reluctantly
4. Remain undecided
5. Have no information/insufficient information

6. Are not able to see a need
7. Need to think it over
8. Consider it the wrong time
9. Have to refer decision to others
10. Are actively supportive

You will need a different strategy depending on what stage the person to be influenced is at.

Be realistic about your chances – it is unlikely that others will move from open disagreement to active support. The best you may achieve is to move them to neutral. But that's a victory!

> *Leadership is the ability to get people to do what they don't want to do, and like it.*

Harry Truman

HANDLING RESISTANCE

COVERT DISAGREEMENT

'Well, OK, if that's what you want.'
Thinks to self: *'What a load of nonsense – I'm not doing that'.*

These people are actively working against you. Gently
transform their energy into a willingness to talk
openly about their concerns. Once you have done
this, you can then:

- Work to build rapport and a positive relationship

- Stress areas of agreement before moving
  onto areas of disagreement

- Use humour and positive anecdotes

- Meet regularly to develop a working relationship

- Respect their position, promote your own

90

HANDLING RESISTANCE

OPEN DISAGREEMENT

'Hmm – it might be possible, but I doubt it ...'

People who disagree need time to come around to your way of thinking.

- Support your statements with proof and evidence
- Use statistics and numbers accurately and appropriately; avoid trickery
- Be clear about areas of agreement and disagreement
- Ask for a little and get it, rather than a lot and be turned down
- Demonstrate ways in which you understand their viewpoint
- Show that you seek a *win-win* outcome

RELUCTANT COMPLIANCE

'Well, if that's what you want that's what we'll have to do.'

Link your point of view to the compliant person's feelings, values and concerns to move him or her towards actively supporting your ideas.

- Stress connections between your proposal or position and the person's interests
- Avoid complex arguments
- Focus on simple and vivid points and benefits
- Be prepared to repeat these in many different forms
- Stress mutual benefits
- Point out mutual losses if your ideas aren't accepted

UNDECIDED

'I'm just not sure it will work.'

Work to tip the scales in your favour.

- Focus on your side of the issue
- Re-state mutual benefits
- Minimise/solve problem issues
- Support your case with expert evidence
- Cite cases where similar proposals or ideas have been successful
- Break your proposal down into small, more acceptable action items
- Follow up (in writing?) to avoid the person slipping back into indecision

NO INFORMATION/INSUFFICIENT INFORMATION

'I need more background information before I can make a decision.'

Find out what information is missing or needed.

- Back it with proof and evidence
- Avoid swamping the other person with too much info
- Invite questions and requests for clarification
- Get the person to agree that the information is sufficient and acceptable
- Make your information lively and attractive

NOT ABLE TO SEE A NEED

'I just don't think we have a need for that right now.'

Acknowledged need is the bedrock of acceptance.

- Conduct more detailed fact-finding
- Get agreement along the way that needs exist
- Ask what may happen if these needs remain unfulfilled
- Illustrate how similar needs have been met for others
- Create a summary of the specific benefits of your suggestion

NEED TO THINK IT OVER

'Hmm – I must give this some thought. Can you come back next month?'

Some people do need time to think things through. Establish what aspects of the idea they need to think about: 'What exactly is it that you want to think over … *(Don't pause here)* … is it x, or y, or z?'.

- Reiterate the main benefits of your proposals
- Clarify any misunderstandings
- Solve any remaining problems or issues
- Make positive use of any delay
- Provide a written summary of your ideas and the benefits

WRONG TIME

'It's a bad time for us to be making decisions like this.'

Assuming this is a genuine reason and not a delaying tactic, you can use waiting time to your mutual advantage.

- Ask when would be an appropriate time
- Use the time delay to road test your ideas, organise a dry run, double check your plans

REFERRING DECISION TO OTHERS

'I'll need to have a word with my partner and come back to you.'

You should already have established that the person you are attempting to influence has the authority to say *yes*.

In which case, ask: 'Are you happy with what I am suggesting?'. If the person is happy, suggest that you *both* take the issue to the higher authority and work as a team to get final agreement.

GETTING A DECISION

WHY IS IT NECESSARY?

Unless the person you are influencing offers an unconditional *yes* to your proposals you will need to do or say something that will generate a positive decision.

Here are two steps you can take towards getting a decision:

1. Ask yourself 'How does this person normally go about making decisions?'. Most people usually have a preferred way of making up their mind. Some people take their time to decide, others are happy to make snap decisions. You can sometimes push the latter, but will need to tread more carefully with the former.

2. Have a variety of ways in which you can stimulate a decision.

GETTING A DECISION

SPOT THE SIGNALS

Knowing when to ask for a decision can be critical. Ask too soon and you may frighten the other person off. Ask too late and you may miss your best chance. Watch for signals that suggest the other person is ready to decide:

- Leaning forward, seeming more interested and involved
- Head up, good eye contact
- Stroking chin thoughtfully
- Nodding or smiling in agreement with you
- Upward inflection in voice tone
- Requesting more information
- Asking you to repeat some points you made earlier
- Making notes
- Asking 'What if ..' or 'Suppose ...' questions
- Checking guarantees, support, follow-up plans
- Picking up your written proposal and double checking aspects
- Discussing implementation details

GETTING A DECISION

DEALING WITH DITHERERS

A good way of avoiding a decision is to say 'I want to think about it.'

Sometimes people do want time to think things through. But, very often, this can be an excuse or a put-off.

Ask:

- 'What exactly do you want to think through? (*Whatever you do - don't pause here!*) Is it the implementation schedule? Is it the bottom line? Is it the timing?'

Once you have isolated the real reason, you are much better placed to respond to the objection.

WAYS & MEANS

Going for yes

● 'If you agree, shall we go ahead right away?'

Its very directness appeals to the proactive leader or creative talker.

If the answer is *no*, ask a *SuperQuestion*: 'What's preventing you from going ahead?'.

WAYS & MEANS

The Alternative Choice Question

This is less direct because you enable
people to make a choice between
two possible options.

- 'When would you like to start – Friday
  or shall we wait until Monday?'

- 'Which of these two do you prefer?'

- 'Which film shall we see – this one, or
  that one?'

GETTING A DECISION

WAYS & MEANS

The Minor Decision

Another soft tactic. Here, you ask people to make a decision about a relatively unimportant aspect of the proposal. If they give the go-ahead, the assumption is that they agree to the whole idea.

- 'Where do you want your logo to appear – at the top of the form or do you think it would look better bottom right?'

- 'By the way, how do you intend to resource the project?'

- 'How should we deal with the Western branches?'

GETTING A DECISION

WAYS & MEANS

The Assumptive Question/Statement

This question/statement works well with the reactive follower and the creative talker, both of whom need a continuous nudge towards decisions. (Be careful with the analytical listener who dislikes presumption.)

- 'After we start I assume you'll want a monthly update?'
- 'You'll notice significant improvements immediately after we start.'

WAYS & MEANS

The Benefit Summary

Some people like to hear a review of the benefits they will receive if they agree to your ideas. A quick list followed by a decision question often does the trick.

- 'OK – let's summarise. After we've made the alterations you will notice that you have extra time available for other things, you'll start to save on budget and you'll have a happier work force. So, shall we go ahead?'

MORE SOURCES & RESOURCES

Films:

Twelve Angry Men

Casablanca

Dead Poets' Society

It's A Wonderful Life

Field of Dreams

The Shawshank Redemption

Books:

'**Words That Change Minds**', Shelle Rose Charvet, ISBN 0-7872-0803-5
'**Influencing with Integrity**', Genie Laborde, ISBN 0-933347-10-3
'**The Magic of Rapport**', Jerry Richardson, ISBN 0-916990-20-6
'**The Art of Persuasive Communication**', Richard Storey, ISBN 0-566-07819-8
'**Influence - science and practice**', Robert B. Cialdini, ISBN 0-321-01147-3

General:

Advertisements
Modelling influential colleagues, friends, neighbours and relations
Politics and politicians; debates and discussions

About the Author

Richard Storey
Richard worked in the newspaper industry before moving into training
and development. He is an internationally known communication
consultant with over 25 years' experience. He has published *The Art of
Persuasive Communication* (Gower 1997) as well as a number of
management and professional workbooks. He is a regular contributor
of articles to magazines and journals. In addition to teaching a range of
communication skills seminars, he is also a regular conference speaker.

Contact
Richard can be contacted at: 23 Gordon Road, Clifton, Bristol BS8 1AW
Tel: 0117 973 2937   E-mail: richardbstorey@btopenworld.com

Published by:
Management Pocketbooks Ltd
Laurel House, Station Approach,
Alresford, Hants SO24 9JH, U.K.
Tel: +44 (0)1962 735573
Fax: +44 (0)1962 733637
E-mail: sales@pocketbook.co.uk
Website: www.pocketbook.co.uk

All rights reserved.   © Richard Storey 2000.
This edition published 2000.   Reprinted 2001, 2003, 2004, 2006.

Design, typesetting and graphics by **efex ltd**   Printed in U.K.

ISBN -10   1 870471 79 2
ISBN -13   978 1 87041 79 4

British Library Cataloguing-in-Publication Data – A catalogue
record for this book is available from the British Library.

ORDER FORM

Your details

Name _____

Position _____

Company _____

Address _____

_____

_____

Telephone _____

Fax _____

E-mail _____

VAT No. (EC companies) _____

Your Order Ref _____

Please send me:

		No. copies
The _Influencing_	Pocketbook	
The _____	Pocketbook	
The _____	Pocketbook	
The _____	Pocketbook	
The _____	Pocketbook	

Order by Post

MANAGEMENT POCKETBOOKS LTD

LAUREL HOUSE, STATION APPROACH,
ALRESFORD, HAMPSHIRE SO24 9JH UK

Order by Phone, Fax or Internet

Telephone: +44 (0)1962 735573
Facsimile: +44 (0)1962 733637
E-mail: sales@pocketbook.co.uk
Web: www.pocketbook.co.uk

MANAGEMENT POCKETBOOKS